HOW TO SEDUCE ANY MAN IN THE ZODIAC

ROBIN MACNAUGHTON

Thorsons

An Imprint of HarperCollinsPublishers

Thorsons
An Imprint of HarperCollins*Publishers*
77–85 Fulham Palace Road
Hammersmith, London W6 8JB

First published by Pocket Books, New York, USA, 1995
Published in the UK by Thorsons 1996
This edition 1998
1 3 5 7 9 10 8 6 4 2

© Robin MacNaughton

Robin MacNaughton asserts the moral right to
be identified as the author of this work

A catalogue record for this book
– is available from the British Library

ISBN 0 7225 3777 8

Printed and bound in Great Britain by
Creative Print and Design (Wales), Ebbw Vale

CONTENTS

Get Him Starry-Eyed…

* Galvanize AQUARIUS with your brilliance. If you turn on his mind he won't care what you're wearing…

* Overwhelm TAURUS' senses with a subtle perfume and a magnificent home-cooked meal. *Forget* him if you'd rather read in bed…

* Dazzle LEO with your beauty and style – but if you're dazzling enough to win him, you'll need to stay that way to keep him…

* Woo VIRGO with an expensive dictionary, not a Cartier tank watch. Remember, he likes cerebral types…

* Invite LIBRA to a chamber concert, then dinner by candlelight. However, a few caveats before you get carried away…

No man is a fortress – when a determined woman breaches the moat! Here's all the wisdom you'll ever need to be Ms. Right to the man of your dreams.

Aries Man

March 21–April 20

What He's Like

He's ardent and enthusiastic, he's impulsive and aggressive. Mr Aries has the personality of a great warrior who wants to set the world on fire. And because he can be so wildly romantic, he may also be able to ignite quite a flame in your heart.

His energy is boundless, his self-assurance astounding. He is a born leader who isn't bashful when it comes to boasting of his achievements. At the same time, he can be both proud and supportive of yours.

Mr Aries has a mind that moves in overdrive. He thinks faster than he can talk, runs rather than walks, and can take on more projects than ten people put together. Whatever he does, from functioning as president of a company to playing tennis, he does it ambitiously.

Essentially, he has an all-or-nothing attitude toward his undertakings. And when he is in his 'all' phase, he can be totally consumed by the emotion of the moment. Whether it's working, loving, or simply living, Mr Aries' passions play a leading role. Even before the world has awakened, he is the knight on a charger galloping toward some intense experience. Anything less would bring on an attack of boredom and make him unfit to be around.

Generally speaking, his personality is impatient, at times temperamental, and often self-serving. Caught in the midst of an impulsive action, he can forget that it is upon people's feelings that he is treading. Mr Aries operates strongly from self-interest and sometimes from sheer selfishness. However, it's precisely his 'me first and perhaps you later' attitude that not only gets him what he wants, but gets it quickly. When caught in the tides of a fulminating temper, he can be truly intimidating to meeker souls. He knows it and uses it to further his goals. But when it works, he is usually too busy beginning something new to even notice.

Not only does he thrive on power, he considers it his divine right. And he's first to admit that probably nobody deserves it as much. At the same time, he can cheerfully drive himself past the kind of limits that would make any normal person pass out from sheer exhaustion. Essentially, Mr Aries loves work, just as he loves to create things – that he can tell other lesser beings how to finish.

He loathes low-energy people, pessimistic souls, and dreary people who would never engage in grand schemes. At the same time, he thrives on power, startling passion, and the feeling of first love, even if it's for the hundredth time. Although Mr Aries can be loyal, his emotional memory does a sudden fade-out when his romantic drama starts to look more like a lengthy documentary. Since he is a man addicted to 'firsts' in record time, his feelings find expression in a new grand love, career goal, or great passion. And each time he will enthusiastically attest that it is just the very best.

Although in the business world he can be tricky and at times manipulative, in romantic relationships he is honest and direct, and expects the same. While nothing makes his pulse race like a good challenge, he also likes his woman of the moment to speak her mind directly. He is much too busy to be bothered with unexpressed feelings or subtle manoeuvres. Therefore, he'll run roughshod over any female who is too timid to tell him what she wants and why. Yet at the same time, she must give him the kind of attention that will assure him that she has the best taste simply because she prefers him. Mr Aries' ego is larger than the Atlantic Ocean. At the same time, it needs to bask in a brilliant sunshine or else he'll see to it that the tide is always out.

What He Thinks He Wants

His favourite things are power and grand passion, and the preferred amount is even more than a lot. Essentially, Mr Aries would like to have total power and recognition in anything he undertakes. And on the side, he would highly appreciate a grand love that would make him feel like his life is a midnight movie minus commercial interruption. Should all of these priorities fail to be immediately forthcoming, he'll simply settle for momentary excitement and a situation in which he stands in command.

What He Needs

His ego is the centre of his universe, and he needs it nurtured daily with large doses of admiration. Aside from that, Mr Aries needs a lot of love, attention, and approval. Sexually, he is insatiable, and he therefore requires someone who can keep up with his habitual forays. Finally, because he can have the fiercest temper, he needs a woman who will not only stand up to him during his more intimidating moments, but who will cool him out during his daily combustions and self-created crises.

What He Fears

This is a most courageous man who not only fears little, but who often finds fearful things exciting. His daring often attracts danger just as his need to push life to the limits can create a lot of havoc. However, if he were to fear anything, it would be the type of rejection that would sabotage his ego and severely compromise his self-esteem. Even when he's wrong, Mr Aries needs to feel that it's so unimportant that if anyone *has* noticed, he or she really shouldn't have.

His Attitude Toward Women, Love, and Sex

He is passion personified and can be so ardent with his affections that he can make a woman feel that she's never been loved before. While he may not follow through with flowers, his feelings are romantic and his emotions intense. When he's in love he can be loyal, loving, jealous, and generally consumed with feeling. Mr Aries is also capable of strings of one-night stands and sex that is more biologic than rhapsodic. Ideally he would love to be in love. However, should that be missing, or even waning, he is not at all shy about seeking his satisfactions elsewhere. Since his sexual energy is so strong that it could probably shatter glass, Mr Aries needs his outlets. Strenuous athletics and a consuming devotion to his career often help. Outside of that, casual sex is something that he is certainly not opposed to. Essentially he is a highly sexed being who has a spontaneous approach – i.e., whoever happens to be turning his wheels at the moment may very soon be in his bed. However, whether she ever sees him after sunrise depends on how intensely she keys into his emotions. When not emotionally involved, Mr Aries can be so cut and dried that he is capable of turning on the news in a moment of afterglow. On the other hand, when he is truly impassioned, he would neither notice nor care if you stopped dieting and gained weight, as long as you gave him a lot of affection.

His Good Points

He is exciting, energetic, strong, courageous, and powerful. He lives his life intensely and without fear. Mr Aries is a man who can make the majority of men seem like weaklings. He has a self-confidence that is contagious and a stellar enthusiasm that is truly magical. His passion for life and love is to be envied, as is his ability to be clear about the desires that he satisfies in record time.

His Bad Points

He can be selfish, egotistical, insensitive, and emotionally capricious. The less-evolved Aries man lives merely for his immediate satisfactions and will tread on the feelings of anyone who might interfere. He sees to it that each person around him has a function that ultimately feeds his feelings of power. And because he is so impatient and temperamental, he'll fail to find the time to show gratitude or appreciation.

How to Get His Attention

Mr Aries responds to high energy, flash, dazzle, and more than a touch of the obvious. He is a sucker for a low-cut blouse, a short skirt, a sexy smile, and conversation centred around him. Therefore, appeal to his baser instincts and approach him. Compliment him on his clothes and say something else with your eyes. Be dynamic, enthusiastic, and very direct. Manoeuvre the focus to his work and make him feel important. Then suggest continuing the conversation over dinner.

How to Keep It

Passion and patience are prerequisite to keeping the fires burning. Sexually, the Aries man is enthusiastic and direct. Sometimes too direct. If you don't tell him what you want, he'll forget to ask. He's got all the instincts of the Ram, but his technique often needs refining. Therefore, he'll supply the energy, but you must supply the imagination. Be warm, affectionate, soothing, and supportive. At the same time, if he in any way tries to bully you, coolly hold your ground. Mr Aries would rather have a woman he can respect, not walk on. On the other hand, that doesn't mean that he won't occasionally try. Firmly make him aware of your feeling and expectations, and should he forget, assertively remind him. Overpower him with physical affection while you make him aware of your special powers. However, at all times let him know that they won't compete with his, and never let him forget it.

Realistic Expectations

Mr Aries is not the easiest man to live with, but he might be one of the most exciting. If you really want him, you must have the self-assurance that you deserve him. At the same time, you must be strong enough to love him without being enslaved by his demands. The only successful relationship with an Aries man is an equal one. If you are ready for the challenge of taming someone who has to be convinced of equality, then you're on the right track to a great love.

Taurus Man

April 21–May 21

What He's Like

He's a highly sensuous man who is a bastion of strength and a buoyant support in moments of crisis. Like his natal element, Taurus is earthy. His approach to life is practical and dependable, and his way of going after what he wants, methodical.

Your Taurus is a patient and persistent soul who takes one thing at a time and hates to be rushed through any experience. Unlike Sagittarius, he requires time to make up his mind and sometimes even more time to take some action.

Mr Taurus has two feet firmly planted in the earth and a mind that is grounded in the material realm. It is likely that he has a special gift for making money as well as a talent for taking care of it. Essentially, he is highly security-conscious, both materially and emotionally. And whether it is in the material or the emotional areas of his life, he will ultimately seek the most stable situation. Beautiful possessions assure him of his power in the world, just as a secure, loving relationship gives his inner life a sense of meaning. However, at times he may confuse the emotional with the material by treating the object of his affections like a possession. When in love, his jealousy is boundless, just as is his need for trust.

Mr Taurus needs to know where he stands before getting emotionally involved. However, when he finally makes up his mind, he remains absolutely certain.

What He Thinks He Wants

He wants sensuality and security, the more of it, the better. However, above all, Mr Taurus wants to be tempted. His greatest fantasy is being seduced, but not abandoned, by a beautiful woman with stellar sex appeal. Next to that, falling in love with someone lovely and enjoying startling material success would make him more than happy.

What He Needs

Whether it's in a material or emotional situation, Taurus needs to feel the support under his feet. Instability unsettles him, as much as the feeling of not knowing where he stands. Security is the key to his existence. Without it, he is tense, anxiety-ridden, and frightened.

What He Fears

He is frightened of anything being pulled out from under him. Like his astrological opposite Scorpio, the Taurus man is fearful of being abandoned. Too little money makes him insecure, along with falling in love with a woman he's not sure of. To survive, Mr Taurus has to know where he stands. And in order to thrive, he has to feel in control of both his circumstances and his options.

His Attitude Toward Women, Love, and Sex

Because his body often rules his brain, Mr Taurus is most eagerly seduced by someone very sensual. He's probably a *Playboy* peruser and has fantasies of being overwhelmed by Wonder Woman. In addition to being a sucker for a pretty face, he's a highly appreciative audience for an attractive body. As a matter of fact, one might say that being enslaved by his senses is probably his very favourite thing.

Mr Taurus is a highly sensual man who loves love, sex, and women. However, unless there are other indications in his horoscope, he is more of a monogamous lover than a playboy. He is most definitely the marrying kind and the kind of man who wants children. In love he not only seeks security, but also gives it willingly. And even if he prefers a living-together situation to a marriage, Mr Taurus will remain very steady and faithful

Unlike a Leo, he doesn't need a lot of surface excitement to nurture his interest. Nor does he need to spend his evenings out on the town. When he is with the person he loves, he would be just as happy to stay home together and eat pizza than spend the evening in an expensive restaurant.

When he really falls in love, Mr Taurus gives himself completely. And of course, he expects the same. Having a highly jealous nature, he will not tolerate sideline flirtations and is capable of becoming violent when confronted with an infidelity. Emotionally, he is a conventional man who doesn't believe in making love complicated. Essentially, he follows his desires, and wherever they take him, he's likely to end up.

His Good Points

He's loyal, loving, and very dependable. Not only is Taurus strong, he's like a mountain in the middle of the ocean. His character is solid, his desires enduring. And when he says he is going to do something, it can be considered done. He is a man who is highly supportive, sensuous, and creative. In addition, it is likely that he is also a good cook. Mr Taurus can make you feel so secure that you'll start to believe in ever after. Basically that's because he does.

His Bad Points

He can be stubborn, rigid, and uncompromising. And when truly unevolved, both cheap and selfish. The less-evolved Taurus man lives his life by rote, with little or no imagination. Not only does he get stuck in ruts, he creates them, without stopping to consider other alternatives. As a result, he can be both boring and confining to be around, especially when he treats each new day exactly like the day before and the day before that.

How to Get His Attention

Appeal to his earthy sensuality. Titillate his senses by smelling beautiful, looking seductive, and cooking him a meal that blows his mind. Mr Taurus craves creature pleasures – from food to sex. And his appetites are usually enormous. Therefore, invite him for an elegant 'home-cooked' dinner – even if you have to take it out. (That's *your* secret.) Serve it with fine French wine on a table set with roses and candlelight. (Ruled by the planet Venus, Mr Taurus loves the trappings of beauty.) Wear a sweet, noticeable scent and a dress that flatters your best assets. After dinner, adjourn to the sofa for talk. He'll take it from there.

How to Keep It

Mr Taurus loves sex, probably even more than he loves food, and probably even more than he loves money. Therefore, any woman who would rather read in bed than do other things is better off forgetting him and simply finding an Aquarius. Since he is highly responsive to sight, touch, and, of course, smell, he will be most attracted to a woman who appeals to all of these. Taurus loves to touch and be touched. If you know how to give a good back rub, you're as good as engaged. Don't be shy to act out your fantasies with this man – his enthusiasm will surprise you. However, unless a woman is either beautiful or sexually magnetic, he can be very slow in making up his mind. Since Mr Taurus tends to be so security-conscious, he may drift into a situation that is comfortable yet not consuming. However, for him to be truly in love, his senses simply have to be overtaken.

Realistic Expectations

When his senses are overwhelmed, or at least catered to, Taurus can be a great lover-husband-friend. He will support you in times of emotional crisis. And he will offer you a love that you can believe in. But in turn you must nurture his need for sensuality, security, and a stable love. In the end, what you will gain is a lover you can trust as a friend.

Gemini Man

May 22–June 21

What He's Like

He's a gregarious, good-time person who loves parties, people, and constant activity. Essentially, Mr Gemini is far more cerebral than emotional and can sometimes be quite insensitive. His personality is maddening, madcap, and invincibly charming. Likewise, his mind is restless, his actions contradictory, and his emotions ambivalent. Basically, he is on an endless quest for the kind of excitement that can make him forget what time it is. Often he finds it in momentary flirtations and fascinating mental pursuits.

What He Thinks He Wants

Since Mr Gemini loses interest easily, he seeks the kind of stimulation that's always as exciting as the first time around. Because he's such a mental being, a mind as clever as his own will provoke an instantaneous need to pursue something further. Not only does he desire someone to talk to, but he also wants to be entertained with witty, pithy instant retorts. That perfectionistic part of him also yearns for a heavy dose of dazzling beauty from some damsel who beckons from afar. Later in life he usually realizes that he can't have everything he wants because he wants everything. Often he'll just settle for the best he can get, give up and get married. Unfortunately, the restlessness often persists and so does the excitement seeking.

What He Needs

Supply him with constant challenges that vary from mind games to serious mental endeavours. This is a character who would by far prefer a string of clever lines to a lot of emotional reassurance. His best match is a woman with a sensational sense of humour who's as cerebral, exciting, and changeable as he is. On any day, he'd rather be offered some exciting new insight than a gigantic piece of home-made pie. Mr Gemini thrives on having his mind stroked by a touch of genius. In lieu of that, sheer intelligence will do. So don't even bother cooking for him. Instead, just laugh a lot and be constantly clever.

What He Fears

He is terrified of being confined. The mere thought of it gives him acute suffocation, indigestion, and probably even insomnia. Even on his slow days, this man moves like quicksilver. However, he'll move even faster if he feels you want to close in on him. In his mind, the only stability is change and the kind of order that he finds in his cheque-book. Don't dare to ask him if he thinks he might like to settle down in six months, or else you're dating your own demise. Most likely he hasn't the vaguest idea of what he's going to want, feel, think, or fear in the next two weeks. And even if he tried hard to work it all out beforehand, it's inevitable that he'd change his mind in the meantime. Lean on him for security and you'll find yourself falling through the air. On the other hand, let him know that you only love him 'in the now' and you may end up keeping him forever.

His Attitude Toward Women, Love, and Sex

He likes women and likes to have a lot of them around him a lot of the time. Mr Gemini is a born flirt. It comes more naturally to him than sleeping or eating. Whether or not he's even conscious of it, his twinkling eyes and sly little grin can create a crowd of female attention. Basically, he's emotionally ambivalent, and while he finds flirtations with women a lot of fun, at the same time he fears that a deeper involvement is a threat to his sense of freedom. And it often is.

Although he abhors jealousy and has a hard time understanding it, his gregarious yet diffident attitude often inspires it. Somehow he can never understand how his friendliness is being interpreted as flirtation and how his flirtations are being fantasized about as potentially deep involvements. Basically, his attitude toward love is that he loves everybody – in different ways, at different times, for different reasons, but always with some distance. Ideally he's most suited for the kind of relationship that gives him the illusion of total freedom while it creeps up on him and gets him from behind. Even then, he's not necessarily going to be faithful. Gemini men are notorious lotharios who are far more intrigued with the novelty of a new person than with the desire for sex or emotional security. Romantically, he can be fickle and has a peculiar way of deadening his own feelings with his mind. Only when he finds the perfect mental enthrallment can he find himself becoming emotionally involved. The key to his sexual passion is what he *thinks* about the person he happens to be making love to. The problem is that often he cannot decide.

His Good Points

He's funny, witty, clever, comical, charming, exciting, inventive, and usually irresistible. He can make you burst out laughing on one of your bad days, and with a simple smile, send you soaring on your good days. His personality is more fun than champagne on a summer afternoon. One hour with him can make you forget that you've ever known boredom.

His Bad Points

He's fickle, erratic, often capricious, and terribly frightened of involvement. One month he may claim that he's fallen in love. The next month he may forget to even call you. His way of getting involved is to keep one foot out the door and his eyes darting about for the sudden appearance of someone more exciting. He tries to translate his feelings into thoughts and ends up extremely confused about what he thinks he's feeling as opposed to what he thinks he wants to feel. Mr Gemini is capable of standing you up, being exceedingly superficial when you want him to be serious, and flirting with other female faces at your own wedding reception.

How to Get His Attention

Since Mr Gemini is a cerebral sort of guy who loves mind trips, what you wear is less important than what you say. So startle him with a witty little line that's guaranteed to make him laugh. Then follow it up with some fascinating fact that leads into sparkling conversation. Capture his mind with your best ability at being clever and then do something unpredictable like walk away. You can reconnect later on, but initially Mr Gemini loves a hide-and-seek sort of challenge. So dazzle him one moment and disappear the next. Let him worry about when he'll get to see you again. This is an easily bored, emotionally detached man who needs to stretch.

How to Keep It

Play it very cool, yet very friendly. Titillate him with trenchant insights about himself and then step back and keep him guessing. He responds well to games – both emotional and sexual – and even thrives on them. Therefore, keep a copy of the *Kama Sutra* and Kierkegaard by the bed (as conversation pieces) since your Gemini is as turned on by your mind as he is by your body. When it comes to being romantic, he is as likely to tell jokes as he is to praise your eyes. He's also likely to tell you about some wonderful new woman he met at the most inopportune moments. So let him feel that you love him in the moment but that you're much too independent and popular to even consider commitment.

Realistic Expectations

Don't start out aiming for connubial bliss, although you may attain it. This is not a man who even understands what is meant by security. Nor does he want to. If you happen to be detached, and more interested in mental stimulation than profound emotional reassurance, then he could very well be for you. However, if you're seeking security, stability, and someone cuddly to come home to, forget it. Essentially, if you can't take him without worrying about what might happen tomorrow, don't take him. If that is your priority, you've already lost what you are looking for.

CANCER MAN

June 22–July 23

What He's Like

Mr Cancer is an enigmatic type of man who may try your emotions and occasionally wilt your self-confidence. He is a highly changeable character, one day playing cool and aloof, the next day being disarmingly sentimental. Because of the continual fluctuation of Mr Cancer's moods, it is sometimes impossible to predict when you really have him. However, when he makes up his mind that he has definitely decided, he will court you with the tenacity of someone out to win a race. When Mr Cancer sets his mind on a goal, there is simply no stopping him. Between the flowers, the dinners, the trips, and the presents, you may feel dangerously overwhelmed. His special way of informing you that he wants you is to treat you like a countess. However, at the same time, he'll let you know that his drama does not include any competition. Just try making him jealous when you happen to be wearing his perfume and you will witness a very sentimental man turn suddenly cold. Emotionally speaking, Mr Cancer simply won't consider second place.

Generally, he expresses his anger by withdrawing, turning glacial, and making you feel guilty. And when he withdraws, his scowl can remind you of a hurricane in the middle of August. That's because his mind is being buffeted about in such a huge emotional storm. And when it will settle down is something of which even he is uncertain.

This is a man who is difficult to understand, never mind really get to know. And in order to begin, you can't take his moods to heart. Mr Cancer will always have his crabby moods and his occasional withdrawals, at the same time that he would rather act indirectly than discuss what's on his mind. It's best during these times to simply walk into another room and forget him. Eventually his eyes will brighten and his subtle sense of humour will return – if only to be eventually overshadowed by another mood.

Mr Cancer takes his feelings super seriously – sometimes far more seriously than he'll take yours. Because he is supersensitive, he tends to nurse slights and get caught in pessimistic places. That is why he needs someone who is not only secure, but also very positive to push him far away from himself.

Emotionally he is highly receptive, but will go to any lengths to avoid showing his vulnerability. Often when he is pouting, he is really hurt or wounded and cannot express it openly. Basically, Mr Cancer is a man who sometimes finds it easier to close off than to get close to a person, despite the fact that his desire may dictate the opposite behaviour.

Security is a key word to his personality, and this most definitely involves money. While he can be generous to a fault, he is driven to make a lot of money since it is only with a sizable sum in back of him that he really feels secure. Emotionally speaking, his security need makes him hunger for a sense of family. Therefore, he is prone to play the roles of both husband and father quite naturally. When he really cares, Mr Cancer can have a strongly nurturing effect on those around him, which makes up for the times when he retreats into his shell, like his astrological symbol, the crab.

What He Thinks He Wants

Mr Cancer wants a nice home, a family, a romantic love, and enough money in the bank to cushion even an economic disaster.

What He Needs

Security is the password to his psyche. And he needs to be assured that he has it. Unlike Gemini, who is continually concerned with what is ahead of him, your Cancer cares about what is in back of him as well as how long it will last. On a very deep level, he needs the bastions of monetary and emotional security as a life support. They not only define the direction of his life, but they also promote his sense of well-being.

What He Fears

First, he fears that he won't be able to establish security. Second, he fears that when he has it, he may lose it.

His Attitude Toward Women, Love, and Sex

Although Mr Cancer is a true romantic, he doesn't fall in love easily. Because he tends to be both shy and sexually unassertive, he is most strongly attracted to self-assured, vivacious women who not only demand what they want, but who are also capable of taking it The complexity of his character is such that as soon as a woman humbly bows to him, he feels like backing off. Romantically speaking, he likes his senses to be overpowered. And when that doesn't happen, he may take an inordinate amount of time in making up his mind.

However, once he does commit himself, his attitudes are quite conventional. Mr Cancer is not only a marrying man, but one who expects to be a father. Then, once he has created a family situation, his sentimental nature will take hold. He will remember all the important holidays and play fatherly protector to his family. Yet even when he is deeply in love, his moods may overshadow romantic situations and make a woman feel like she's living with a man who is several people. She is. Anyone who marries a Cancer must be prepared for the fact that each side of his personality will always play a part in her life.

His Good Points

He can be kind, sensitive, protective, and sympathetic. In addition, he can be both perceptive and intuitive. Mr Cancer not only has an innate shrewdness with money, but he is often extremely generous. When in love, he will be both loyal and loving. His sentiment is boundless and his feelings both profound and sincere.

His Bad Points

He can be passive and cowardly, fearful and weak. Mr Cancer can have terrible problems when it comes to confronting a situation, and will sometimes let things slide rather than simply taking charge. His sullen and cantankerous moods can be overwhelming. In addition, pessimistic attitudes sometimes overshadow his life.

How to Get His Attention

Shy, insecure, and highly self-protective, Mr Cancer can be a complete puzzle to the woman who gets pushed around by his defences. At first he may appear cold, but actually his coldness is masking an immense insecurity. Trust is his key issue. Therefore, to captivate him you have to make him forget himself – his little worries, his petty fears, his need for self-defence. He responds most readily to intensely vivacious women who carry him along with their joy and laughter. Look like you're someone who loves life and doesn't mind sharing the secret, and he'll be intrigued.

Approach him in an offhand manner. Be witty, playful, and lightly touch him on the arm for emphasis when you talk to him. Cancer is a sensual sign that needs touch just as much as it needs love. Appeal to those needs through scent, body language, and a basic reassuring attitude that tells him that this is an attraction you want to take further.

How to Keep It

Be strong, sensual, and very supportive. Mr Cancer is most intensely attracted to assertive, self-assured women who win his sense of respect. In addition to that, he loves to be complimented, wooed and nurtured. Therefore, keep the romance in the relationship and let him know that it's totally in response to the feelings he arouses in you. Since Mr Cancer loves to feel seduced even if he is the one seducing, make him feel that your life together is one great love affair. Sheer negligees, candlelight in the bedroom, scented sheets, and fresh flowers will keep his libido high. If you're daring, massage oil would not be out of the question. This man loves to be stroked. Be gentle with him; overwhelming animal passion is not his style, though he can be a tender and considerate lover. Finally, allow him his space when his moods overwhelm him. And even on his crabby days, let him feel appreciated, cherished, and deeply loved.

Realistic Expectations

Mr Cancer does best with a woman who's so strong that she gives rather than seeks emotional support. Although he is a sentimental man, he can still be surprisingly cold if a woman has not won his respect. Therefore, desiring him is not enough. First you have to show him that you're so special that you deserve him. If you can do that, you'll probably have him forever.

Leo Man

July 24–August 23

What He's Like

At his best, he's strong and dignified, emotional and romantic. When he's on, Mr Leo has a personality that can charm serpents. Because of his warmth and wit, optimism and enthusiasm, his presence is a plus in all social situations. At the same time, his stellar sex appeal, self-assurance, and sense of glamour can make women forget that there are other men residing on the same planet.

Mr Leo is a flirt who usually feels happiest when he is the centre of attention. He is especially fond of women who not only flatter him, but who make him look good by association. He can be a snob who is easily seduced by the props of money, glamour, and power, and is capable of placing superficial values over serious human considerations.

The key to his psyche is his ego. Mr Leo is easily flattered and can be fooled by insincere compliments, since basically he wants to believe them. His pride is consuming and can lead him to confuse personal feelings with impersonal issues.

Usually he is energetic, athletic, ambitious, and power-driven. Not only does he want to make it to the top, he also wants to own it. Whether it's in the bedroom or the boardroom, Mr Leo needs to be the boss. At times he suffers from a king complex and tends to treat the people who surround him like servants. He can behave as if, by divine right, he deserves all. And quite often he manages to attain it.

What He Thinks He Wants

He wants everything he can get, the bigger and grander the better. Power, prestige, money, and material success are great for starters. In terms of love, he prefers beauty, glamour, charm, sex appeal, and a personality that is supportive to his ego. Mr Leo seeks to see his more favourable self reflected in the eyes of his lover. At the same time, the woman has to make him look good by her poise, appearance, power, personality, or position. However, the problem is that if she looks too good, suddenly nobody is paying attention to *him*. And that eventually makes Mr Leo somewhat insecure. The most masculine Leo man is simply a little baby at heart. At times, the child in him is charming. However, when his demands become decidedly infantile, he is not only impossible to please, but impossible to love.

He thrives on love and the energy of romance. But when it starts to lose its lustre, he is quite capable of shifting his attention elsewhere. At times, though he thinks he wants more mature love, he's really seeking emotional drama. Scenes of steamy sensuality go straight to his heart. And if there are enough props to give the illusion that this is a great love, his mind, spirit, and body are totally captured.

Next to a grand love, fame, and power, what he thinks he wants most is tranquillity, peace, and security, supported by romantic props and creature comforts. At all times, a highly attractive woman who murmurs in dulcet tones and who looks up to him even if she has to sit down is one of his most essential pleasures. However, Mr Leo is a demanding man, who, unless he happens to be extremely mature, is capable of taking all of his essential pleasures for granted the moment the scene becomes sedentary.

What He Needs

He needs constant attention from a woman who will not interfere with his freedom. He also needs to have his ego stroked. Since Mr Leo thinks in superlatives, he tends to expect a lot. Although he may spend the weekend working his way to the top, he can feel unbelievably abandoned should his lover leave him for an evening to live her life. From a woman, he needs both praise and devotion. However, in turn, he doesn't always want to deal with her demands on his time. Because at any given moment, there are so many things he is not only doing but wants to do, time can become his key obsession. Therefore, what he seeks is a woman who will attend to all his needs while she's careful not to crowd him with hers. And because he has such a charming way of appearing romantic, sexually magnetic, and breathlessly compromised, he usually not only finds her, but keeps her.

What He Fears

Failure of any kind frightens him. Next to that, he panics at the thought that he might not make it to the top quite as quickly as expected. Mr Leo cannot bear rejection of any kind. Nor can he stand feeling insecure. Being jealous by nature, romantically he fears not only the loss of love, but equally important, the loss of attention. At a party, make him feel like he's nothing but another face, and you will probably never see him again. Rip away at his sense of self-respect and you will notice his claws emerge. Threaten his dignity and you will see the fire in him turn to ice. Challenge his security and you will be opening the door for him to make his ultimate departure.

His Attitude Toward Women, Love, and Sex

Mr Leo is a natural flirt who thrives on female attention. However, when his emotions are really aroused, he is capable of abandoning himself wholeheartedly.

He is the classic romantic who can make a woman feel like Cleopatra. Fresh flowers, perfume, champagne, and candlelit dinners are only some of the props that are part of his repertoire. His emotions are sentimental and his spirit generous. However, because he is so discriminating, there are not that many female faces who ignite such intense feeling.

He tends to be a snob who searches for a perfect appearance with a lot of warmth. Basically, he has a special weakness for glamorous, vivacious women who improve his self-image through association.

Marriage is usually a must, since he seeks a partner to play back to him the drama of his life. Once married, he will be strong, supportive, and sometimes bossy when confronted with connubial conflicts. Mr Leo is a natural father who often plays that role with his wife as well as his children. As a husband, he tends to be faithful unless his marriage is bad or becoming boring. And at that point, he's quite capable of cavorting on the side with some seductive beauty.

However, when the chemistry is really working, he'll remember birthdays, anniversaries, sentimental meetings, and maybe even Halloween. Next to being famous, his favourite thing is falling in love. Essentially, he would like to live a life that is like a romantic dream or, at the very least, a compelling drama. And love is the energy that makes it all move.

His Good Points

His charisma, poise, and sheer sex appeal can arrest your sensibilities. At the same time, his strength and masculinity will creep right into your soul. You may feel overpowered by his sense of romance as well as by the fact that you some-how have fresh flowers in every room. He is optimistic, magnanimous, generous, and sentimental. He loves life, beauty, and the best that the earth has to offer. Mr Leo is the classic super-achiever, who has uncanny ways of getting what he wants. His extraordinary creativity will stun you; his drive and determination may make you feel that you've never worked hard. He thinks in superlatives, engages in grand schemes, and optimistically picks up the pieces should everything shatter. At times, it may seem as though his brain is plugged into a sunbeam. No one can be so posi-tive for so long. No one perhaps except Mr Leo, whose sheer vitality and life force make him invincible.

His Bad Points

If he is the lower type, he can be childish, bossy, domineering, self-centred, arrogant, and temperamental. He wants his needs to be gratified immediately, if not sooner, and unfortunately he has a lot of needs. Although he'll prefer that you be independent, he'll still want you to drop what you're doing at his beck and call. And if you're foolish enough to accede to this situation, it's likely that you won't get a thank you. Essentially, he sees all issues from his point of view, and that point of view is his own self-interest. Therefore, his idea of compromise is that you do what he wants and simultaneously show him that you appreciate his idea. His is a restless nature that expects constant attention and entertainment. When it starts to slow down, his desires may drift elsewhere. Mr Leo is quite capable of infidelity just as he is capable of falling out of love. Initially he may be attracted to a woman far more for her body than her mind. And when the flames start to extinguish because he's become very bored, the relationship recedes to mere security, infidelity, or an abrupt parting of the ways. Often he doesn't understand that he's played an active role in a bad situation. It's the other person who is not perfect and who has to understand the parameters of his patience and the importance of his needs. When Mr Leo is bad, it's because he has yet to grow up and take responsibility for his actions. Although he wants to be treated like a king, he can behave like a hungry baby. And because he can charm those around him to get what he wants, he sometimes remains the child while he secretly suffers because of it.

How to Get His Attention

A sucker for snob appeal, Mr Leo wants a woman worthy of him. Therefore, if you are famous, a flawless beauty, or from a royal blood line, all you have to do is show up. However, in lieu of such larger-than-life attributes, look stunning, flash him a queenly smile, and ask him a lot of questions about his favourite subject – himself. While you appear fascinated by every answer, assiduously detail the glossiest aspects of your own bio. (He *loves* to be impressed.) Then invite him to a black-tie ball (or some suitably glamorous occasion) where you shine.

He'll be so dazzled by your style that he'll try to outdo you. Now the fun begins because, always thinking big, he'll be at his best.

How to Keep It

Cater to his needs at the same time that you appeal to his instincts. At all times, look your best and be your wittiest. To begin with, wear silk and serve him champagne and lobster. Over candlelight, hold his gaze and tell him why he's so irresistible. Appeal to his sensuality by being alluring and seductive. Then, in a very feminine way, let him know that he turns you on. This is a man who loves drama. Making mad, passionate love on the beach is more exciting than slinky nightgowns and satin sheets. Therefore, what really matters here is feeling – yours for him, and no one else (even if it's not true). So if he is only half responding, make him think that you've shifted your affections to someone at least as wonderful. Then if he wants you enough that he's willing to fight for you, he'll instantaneously emerge from his detachment. However, should he talk about friendship, forget it. This is clearly not a love that is here to stay.

Realistic Expectations

If you're dazzling enough to win him, you must stay dazzling enough to keep him. Gaining weight and wearing sloppy T-shirts just won't do it. However, although he is highly responsive to the props, what he really wants most is to feel appreciated. Never nag, badger, or whine. Instead make enthusiastic suggestions and keep pleasantly to the point should he counter with a veto. Even when fighting, don't forget his ego. Calling him a jerk will not only make you lose your point, it may make him lose his love. Mr Leo may admit that he is wrong, but he can't bear to be disparaged. Treat him like a king, but never let him forget that you're also a queen, and what could come of it is a lot of love.

VIRGO MAN

August 24– September 23

What He's Like

He's shy and unassuming, critical and pragmatic. Essentially, Mr Virgo is far more analytical than sentimental, and intellectual than romantic. He has both a passion for order and an infinite capacity for detail. And at times, this can consume his life.

His attitudes are somewhat sanctimonious and his approach to life puritanical. This is basically because he cares what people think. Therefore, he is exceptionally concerned with right and wrong, good and bad, and how he appears to the world.

Because he assigns so much power to the opinions of other people, his behaviour conforms to a set of standards that will favourably define him. And one of these standards is a woman who will make him look good, However, unlike Mr Leo, his ideal is not predicated upon physical appearance, but rather upon intellectual achievement and personal power. Since Mr Virgo has such a poorly developed sense of self, he especially seeks someone he can humbly admire. In lieu of this, he will be satisfied with a warm, practical woman who assures him of a sense of security, while she in no way detracts from his self-image.

Even though in theory he would like to love, Mr Virgo may put his emotional needs in the background while he devotes himself wholeheartedly to his work. He tends to be a workaholic whose motivation stems far more strongly from approval needs than from a drive for power. Because his mind is highly disciplined, he has an uncanny way of turning off his feelings to free his thoughts. And likewise he will easily sacrifice both sleep and momentary pleasure to ge a job done well. Therefore, he may be accused of compartmentalized thinking and, generally speaking, would never win an award for either his sense of spontaneity or his unconventional attitudes. His sense of duty is so ingrained that at times it might make him appear more mechanical than human. However, at the same time, when confronted with a person in need, his personality is kind, caring, and extremely solicitous.

Because he tends to be perfectionistic and, at the very least, highly discriminating, Mr Virgo seldom finds his romantic ideal. And even if he does so, he'll try very hard to find some flaws. Since he has such a hard time accepting himself, he can't be comfortable when it comes to accepting other people. Therefore, in insidious ways, he seeks to control the women who get close to him.

Control is a key factor to his personality. Not only does it form the basis of his obsessive need for order, but it also lends him a sense of security that he could probably never fully find in love.

What He Thinks He Wants

Basically, Mr Virgo is looking for perfection. And even if he found it, he would suggest a few improvements. However, in terms of a woman, perfection for him has less to do with physical appeal than with intelligence, emotional strength, and charisma. Essentially, he wants a woman he can respect. And in order to respect her, he has to be intellectually stimulated by her. Stupidity repels him, as does mental, emotional or moral weakness. Likewise, because he is a man who cares a lot about what others think, he places a tremendous emphasis on dignity, poise, and self-possession. Essentially, what he wants most is to love someone he can look up to. However, because he is so critical, it is rare that Mr Virgo finds that perfect person. Instead, he ends up settling for someone comfortable whom he tries his best to improve.

What He Needs

Order and control are prerequisites to his existence. However, unlike Scorpio, who creates a network of controls as protection from his deeper feelings, Virgo's motivation for control is mental. Essentially, he is always thinking about what other people are thinking of him. And because he desires so intensely that the impression be favourable, he is especially careful about how he appears. He finds drunkenness and violent emotional displays vulgar, just as he shies away from scenes of open sentiment. Control gives him a sense of order in his life, which in turn gives him a sense of security. And it is security that is his deepest need. Security for Mr Virgo comes in being able to think quickly, put his feelings on hold, and coldly take charge of a situation that might be shattering around him. Although he will find comfort and pleasure in a warm, stable relationship, in terms of security, he looks only to his own intelligence and self-control. Second to this control, a semblance of order is necessary to his sense of well-being. Without his tidy piles, well-organized files, and bills that are paid promptly, Mr Virgo would be an even more anxiety-ridden man than he is normally.

What He Fears

Even more than love, the most important thing to a Virgo man is his pride in his performance. And what he fears most is feeling that he has failed and looks like a fool. In all life situations he is concerned with his self-image. Therefore any circumstance, person, or place that may threaten it will instigate his instinctive retreat. Although on the surface he seems strong because he is so disciplined, in reality Mr Virgo is very meek. He is a born worrier who has been know to nurse slights that are sometimes self-invented. At the same time, he lacks the courage to confront his offenders and becomes cold and withdrawn as a measure of control. When caught between a relationship conflict and the demands of his work, there is really no contest. Mr Virgo will always choose his work, because a good performance will enhance his appearance. On the other hand, an emotional issue is precarious as well as painful, unless, of course, he can convince his lover that she happens to be wrong.

His Attitude Toward Women, Love, and Sex

Unless he has prominent Leo or Libra planets, this is a man who is not romantic. Rather, he is the classic pragmatist who would, by far, prefer a computer to a Cartier tank watch. Although he won't object to candlelit dinners, he would never think to create them, and would just as soon grab a bite in a coffee shop as go through all the fuss of a French restaurant. Essentially, Mr Virgo is a man who is comfortable with common means as long as he has enough money to support his mental pursuits.

When it comes to women, he needs far less of a glamour girl and more of a woman he can enjoy talking to. Because he is so insecure, he seeks a woman secure enough with herself to make him feel comfortable. However, to fall madly in love, he has to be mentally swept away by someone so intelligent and competent that she gains the golden gift of his respect.

Generally speaking, Mr Virgo is both shy and diffident when it comes to meeting women and showing his emotions. Likewise, he is acutely uncomfortable with intense emotional displays. Therefore, he is best suited to someone more cerebral than emotional, who will treat all emotional conflicts with calm analysis.

Because he is more of the shy, studious type than the pleasure-loving playboy, monogamous relationships are to his advantage. Once in a relationship, he may be both controlling and fault-finding with things that seem to be of minor importance. However, at the same time, he has a hard time taking criticism and allows his ego to get easily bruised over unimportant issues.

On the positive side, he can be loyal, quietly loving, and very caring. He is the kind of man who will be by your side when you are sick and who will willingly go out of his way should you need a favour. At the same time, he demands the deepest loyalty, and witnessing the most harmless flirtation will make him turn abruptly cold. Although he will go to any extent to mask it, Mr Virgo is intensely jealous and needs at all times to be made to feel secure.

Sexually, he tends to be earthy and animalistic, while emotionally he can be uptight, rigid, and puritanical. Generally speaking, Mr Virgo is not your basic fun person, but he *is* someone who will probably stick around. And for a cerebral woman searching for security rather than feverish romance, he could provide a very workable relationship.

His Good Points

He's intelligent, thoughtful, kind, loyal, and very responsible. Although he may be attracted to your body, he is a man who is far more appreciative of your mind. And when he walks out the door and says, 'I'll call you,' you'll probably hear from him the following day. It's possible that Mr Virgo invented follow-through.

His Bad Points

He can be self-righteous and sanctimonious, critical and petty. Minor problems obsess him, as do order, cleanliness, and control. Especially when angry or haughtily disapproving, he can be cold, distant, and uncommunicative. In a serious conflict he is capable of closing his mind to the other side and seeing only his own sensitivities. He will bear grudges and nurse slights with relish. At his worst, he is so lacking in courage and spontaneity that he is confining and boring. And because he places such importance on the opinion of the world at large, he will weakly pander to people in power and behave obsequiously just to salve his fragile self-image.

How to Get His Attention

Because he is so shy, Mr Virgo is relieved if you take the first step, but do it in a way that appeals to his perfectionistic nature. He tends to be serious and interested in self-improvement and practical knowledge. Therefore, competence, fitness, and a well-informed philosophy on life are initial attention getters. Virgos love a slender silhouette, so keep an eye on your figure. He is conservative in taste, so look trim and tastefully chic, and initiate an intelligent conversation about anything from cookery to Buddhist philosophy. The more you know and love to learn, the more he'll be impressed. However, Mr Virgo is also full of opinions himself. So get him going, then let him suggest where you continue the conversation.

How to Keep It

Make him at ease with himself while you massage his ego. And at all times make him feel emotionally secure. If Mr Virgo feels like he's competing with a football field of men, he'll crawl off to his study with a very big book. Stay well informed either in his interests or your own and initiate intellectual discussions that last the night. Also, because he tends to be health- and diet-conscious, watch your weight and remember to exercise. If he notices your thighs look like cottage cheese, he'll also let you know that he's noticing. Because your Virgo is basically shy, a subtle but direct approach is best. Touch his knee to make a point and brush his hair from his forehead. Then let your hand linger a little longer than necessary. Finally, in the event of a fight, never badger, scream, or bring up an emotional issue in public. That will only win you his cold glance of death, which is guaranteed to make you feel that not only does he not love you, but that you're so worthless that probably nobody else could either. Therefore, deal with emotional differences as if they were intellectual discussions and you're guaranteed to keep him on your side.

Realistic Expectations

If you happen to be looking for a life of glamour, passion, and excitement, you probably won't find it here, unless he happens to have prominent Leo or Libra planets. However, if you desire a quiet, stable, orderly existence with someone who may nag you about balancing your chequebook, then Mr Virgo just may be for you. However, keep in mind that even if this is a marriage made in heaven, its roots are very much in the earth.

THE

LIBRA MAN

September 24– October 23

What He's Like

He has a quiet kind of charm and a very mellow exterior. Underneath he may be emoting heavily. However, at the same time, his façade can appear cool, relaxed, and aloof.

Essentially, Mr Libra is an interesting blend of the mind and the emotions. A part of him is sentimental and sensual at the same time that another part is ruled by reason. His mind is so thoughtful that it sometimes interferes with his feelings. Yet his feelings always find their way to the surface. And although he may suffer from emotional confusion, he is always conscious of his conflicts as well as of his choices.

He is affectionate and romantic, refined yet pleasure-loving. Even his sybaritic tendencies are displayed with style. Beauty makes the muscles of his heart move, as does the right kind of romance. Essentially, he is an ethereal romantic who is in love with love or at least with the splendour of the emotion. When properly motivated, he can supply the props for the most resplendent kind of love. However, he needs a woman who in some way is as scintillating as his props or else his original dazzle may abruptly disappear.

The more lowly evolved Libran is superficial and more interested in a façade than in deeper feelings. He is fickle, capriciously changeable, and maddeningly indecisive. As a lover he is flirtatious, inconstant, yet devastatingly charismatic. At the same time he can also be quite selfish and very undependable.

The more highly evolved Libran is dependable and devoted, sincere and sympathetic. He seeks to play out his need for romance in a more mature kind of love. And as long as this love remains satisfying, he never ceases to appreciate both it and the woman who has helped it happen.

What He Thinks He Wants

Mr Libra loves romance, the more rhapsodic the better. He nurtures the dream of the perfect love and has a special weakness for all the props that go along with it. Candlelight, good music, fine food, wine, and wafts of perfume carry him away. However, there is nothing that he responds to as intensely as physical beauty. Therefore, he is easily enslaved by a pretty face, especially if it's packaged with a poised personality, and even more so if it comes with a keen intelligence. It is not that Libra is critical, it is simply that he is a romantic idealist who longs for the perfect love story. Beauty is intrinsic to his sense of well-being. Therefore, his first priorities, perhaps even before brains and character, are a face and body that he likes to look at.

His Attitude Toward Women, Love, and Sex

Falling in love with love is probably his favourite thing. However, staying in love can be quite another matter.

Because Mr Libra genuinely likes women, he is an easy prey to their beauty and their charm. Unless he is the highly evolved Libra type, he can be compulsively unfaithful. However, unlike Gemini, it is not a need for variety that consumes him. Rather it is a momentary weakness that makes him forget what time it is. Caught in the snare of a beautiful, crafty woman, he may claim later on that he never knew what hit him. It might also be added that he probably didn't want to know.

The more highly evolved Libra usually suffers at the hands of some insensitive beauty early on in life. And he uses this experience in his later years to thoughtfully evaluate what he really wants from love. As he grows older, he puts a serious value on all relationships and enters into them with a commendable sense of equality. He is the kind of man who will either help with the housework or suggest hiring a maid. He will bring you flowers every other day and then celebrate the anniversary of the moment that he met you. He can bring you the kind of romance that you've only read about. However, for him to be so madly motivated, his emotions have to be swept away.

Even the most highly evolved Libra man likes pretty women who know how to make the most of their looks.

Ugliness oppresses him, as does any form of crudeness or vulgarity. Likewise, he is totally turned off by temper tantrums and hysterics. Essentially, he sees relationship problems as conflicts and feels that conflicts should be resolved by calm communication. Screaming disrupts his sense of harmony and strongly unsettles his nerves. That doesn't mean that he may never do it. It does mean that it makes him feel unnatural and out of control.

He has a strong sensuality that is an extension of his emotional sensitivity. However, while the highly evolved Libra man may provide the apogee of physical passion, the more immature type is often passive, self-centred, and sexually insecure. Generally Mr Libra's sensuality extends to everything around him, from his love of music, fine food, wine, fresh flowers, and exotic smells to his finely developed sense of colour.

Physically, he is affectionate and likes to express his feelings best through touching. Essentially, Mr Libra takes sex just as seriously as he takes love. In these two areas he seeks the perfect sensation and the most acute emotion. Therefore, any woman who is more cerebral than sensual will neither captivate him nor be terribly compatible.

Because Mr Libra thinks in terms of 'we' rather than 'I', he is happiest with a partner. Generally, he enjoys shared experience far more than solitary endeavours. The closeness and security provided by a harmonious romantic marriage are the meaning that could make the most of his life.

His Good Points

His sense of romance can make you feel like you're living with the Great Gatsby. He'll shower you with affection, fresh flowers, champagne, and perhaps poetry. He is caring yet not confining, loving yet not mawkishly sentimental. His languid sensuality is a guaranteed turn-on. At the same time, his sensitivity goes straight to your soul. At his best, he's a gentleman whose poise and impeccable manners are even more than refreshing. His personality is charming and his wit arresting. His mind is intelligent, deliberate, creative, and thoughtful. Even when it goes against his own self-interest in a conflict, Mr Libra tries to appreciate the opposing side. Therefore, he is easy to communicate with and quick to understand. Because he is so responsive to beauty and pleasure, he can be very exciting company. Essentially Mr Libra is an intense lover who is also a very good friend. And any way you look at it, that's a lot.

His Bad Points

He can be the number one playboy on the planet earth. And a man who is more interested in your measurements than in your emotions. He can be a slave to his thirst for beauty and a hopeless prisoner of his self-indulgent desires. He has a special weakness for divine highs and beautiful bodies. The more of all of the above, the better. Therefore, he can fall blissfully in love in one week, and three months later decide that the thrill is gone, bells are no longer ringing, and that there are other enticing bodies begging to be explored.

Not only can he be emotionally fickle, but he often feels sorry for himself when he suffers because of it. He can also be so evasive when it comes to emotional confrontations that you may feel that you have to have him kidnapped to instigate honest communication. At his worst, he is passive and indecisive, emotionally confused and very insecure.

Mr Libra can be a dependent man who needs a lot of emotional support, yet in turn is capable of abandoning you for someone he considers more beautiful. This lower type of Libran man seeks momentary rapture rather than mature love. And the fascinating thing is that he always seems to find it.

What He Needs

He needs beauty, harmony, and security. Squalor and dirt depress him profoundly and affect his overall functioning. Likewise, a sense of harmony in his surroundings keeps Mr Libra balanced while beauty helps him thrive. However, what he needs most is the beauty and intensity that come from a close, trusting, equal relationship based on sexual compatibility, similar interests, and mutual respect.

What He Fears

Although he seldom shows it on the surface, underneath, Mr Libra is rather insecure. His deepest fear is being abandoned or romantically betrayed. Next, he fears growing old alone – and that he may never find the right person to perfect his fantasy of woman.

How to Get His Attention

Mr Libra loves beauty above all else. Appearance is everything to him, so if your surface doesn't beguile him, you'd better give up from the start. Perfect grooming is a must. Mr Libra will be the first to notice sloppy little flaws and signs of poor maintenance. So look your most perfect and invite him to a Sunday afternoon chamber concert. (Mr Libra has a great aesthetic sensibility.) Afterward, at supper, discreetly excuse yourself to touch up your perfume and makeup. Then, as you dine over candlelight, speak so softly that he has to lean forward to hear you and will thus be entranced by your scent.

How to Keep It

Appeal to his senses. Spray Chanel No. 5 on your sheets, and at all times look your most beautiful. Serve him flaming dinners by candlelight with Brazilian jazz playing in the background. On grey, rainy afternoons, make a champagne brunch and then kiss him slowly on the neck when he least expects it. And above all, never let him witness the behind-the-scenes work that goes into your glamour performance. In the event of a fight, communicate without screaming. If you seriously disrupt his sense of harmony, you will be shattering the love you have between you. This is a man who may not agree with you, but who will try his best to understand. Give his good intentions the benefit of the doubt while you make him aware of your needs. Then offer reasonable insights into how he might meet them. And instead of accusing him of failing to make you happy, calmly communicate how he can better the situation.

Realistic Expectations

He's a born flirt who simply can't help himself. Mr Libra even charms dogs, children, and little old ladies. However, if he is the evolved Libran, he's also capable of being totally devoted. When he is in love or even strongly attracted, he will provide more than his share of the romance. He'll also volunteer to help you with the dishes and may outdo you with the cooking, too. Basically, he is a sensitive, caring person who seeks meaning in life through the experience of a partner. Therefore, he is open to creating a long-lasting relationship. However, if he is the unevolved type, who is weak, confused, and enslaved by his insecurities, he is capable of leaving you for a teenager after twenty years of marriage. Therefore, critically decide which direction he's coming from before you get carried away.

SCORPIO MAN

October 24– November 22

What He's Like

He operates on many levels simultaneously. Therefore, he's many things at once most of the time. He's the most complex character in the zodiac and can be as enigmatic as a Chinese riddle. It takes a female mind as convoluted as his own to understand him, and that is because there is only so much understanding that can come from communication. To know him profoundly, you have to intuit his total behaviour. And because there aren't that many people whose minds are moulded in the same way, he remains largely misunderstood. And this, he often uses to his advantage.

One hour with him and you know he's dangerous. It's in his eyes. They either gleam like polished weapons or they flicker like serpents' tongues. With one piercing glance he sees all, while in a entire evening, he allows you to see very little.

The Scorpio man is mysterious. Often to himself as well as to others. He seldom communicates directly and usually resorts to talking in code. Often when making one declarative statement, he means another. Therefore, whoever takes him at face value may never know what he is *really* saying. It is not that he tries purposely to obfuscate issues, it's just that he has a particular knack for making life more complicated.

Although cool on the surface, he is the most intense type of fellow and sometimes wears himself out with all of his self-created dramas. When it is a matter of either pride or passion, he can brood, sulk and obsess up a storm. At the same time, he will go to ridiculous lengths to appear as though there is nothing bothering him. Mr Scorpio does not like to reveal himself until he feels totally secure in a situation. And until he feels assured that he is in total control he never feels secure in any situation.

Quite often he sublimates his sexuality through a consuming devotion to his work. In choosing to escape from disturbing emotional issues, he can be the classic workaholic. Likewise, in choosing to escape from the tedium of life and his own anger, he can become the classic alcoholic. However, although Mr Scorpio may drink excessively, he also has extraordinary will-power and, being a person prone to extremes, may decide at a certain point in his life not to drink at all.

Because his mind is shrewd, his perceptions trenchant, and his memory dangerous, he is best suited for a profession in which success is merely a matter of outwitting his opponents. This he can do drunk, half-dead, or with his eyes half-closed. The problem is that he is so facile with mind games that he often forgets where to stop. As a child, he probably manipulated his mother for a glass of milk because he never thought to simply ask her. As an adult, he cannot fall in love without scheming, conniving, and creating an emotional atmosphere in which he is in control. Often he is moody and depressed because he exhausts himself at being so tricky. Only when skiing, sailing, or enjoying other athletic pursuits can he succumb to the luxury of simple pleasure.

What He Thinks He Wants

His blood boils for the kind of passion that takes his breath away. Essentially the deepest part of him is in search of sexual ecstasy, while the most logical part prefers control. Therefore, he tends to be at war with himself, even when he finds his fantasy situation. However, fortunately for his mental health, those memorable moments do not happen frequently.

This is primarily because his version of great passion is closer to emotional enslavement than simple sex, and this man is not easily emotionally enslaved. Unconsciously, he distinguishes between sex and passion. Sex is an act that is pleasurable; passion, an emotion he'll end up paying for. When he finds himself cavorting in its throes, it's like falling into space with the assurance that an important part of him is either dying off or being devoured.

What brings this all about is too complex for him to simply sort out with his intellect. However, the early signals may start with a lot of steamy eye contact embellished by some trenchant quiet talk. Whatever the symptoms, the key word is *power*. The woman who will make him lose sleep, or at least a lot of lucid moments, has to not only sense it, but assert it. And in order to do that, she has to be self-confident, sexually magnetic, and able to see past his mind games straight through to his soul. With those elements present, he is beyond being attracted: He is bewitched. And that is his favourite feeling, except that it makes him so terrified that he is often tempted to run.

This is a man who is not easy. That is primarily because what he really wants most, he most deeply fears, Therefore, he thinks he wants something else. That something is a close, stable relationship that is secure and will allow him a certain measure of control. Emotionally speaking, this is a much tidier situation than being drunkenly in love and walking into walls. However, the problem is that cosiness isn't quite as colourful. Therefore, often well into middle age, Mr Scorpio sometimes seeks to satisfy both requirements. He has been known to lose himself in the wonders of passion while there is someone waiting patiently at home. To live such a life requires not only a lot of sexual energy, but also a lot of imagination. And he has it.

What He Needs

The three prerequisites in his life are security, control, and power. Although he also needs passion, he can live through periods without it. Because his need for security is so profound, he is a man who always marries, often unhappily, and sometimes many times. Even if it makes him miserable, he will stay in a bad marriage long after it's essentially over, leaving it only for another emotionally secure relationship. However, instead of divorcing, most Scorpio men prefer to operate out of their marriage like an office, while they see another woman on the side. That way, they are doubly secure. Security is essential to their nature, because without it, there can be no control, and without control there can be no sense of power. And it is this sense of power, which comes from being in control of himself as well as of everybody else, that makes Mr Scorpio's pulse race.

What He Fears

He hates being put out of control in any situation and will plot, scheme, and manipulate to avoid it. He also has a deep-seated fear of abandonment, which falling in love often brings about. In addition, an obsession with death can occasionally consume him.

His Attitude Toward Women, Love, and Sex

Sexually, he is a predator, who slowly strolls around his victim before finally circling in for the kill. However, should he sense rejection once he makes his move, he can quickly turn hostile and surly. Usually his approach is cool, cleverly offhand, carefully calculated, and quietly charming. If he is truly attracted, he can sit back and outwait all opposition. Mr Scorpio is a most successful game player who often sets up situations to entrap the woman he wants. However, should his game fail to get the desired response, he withdraws coolly and quietly.

Although he enjoys women, in an entire lifetime he will probably feel close to very few. Regardless of his outward personality, emotionally he is an introvert who has problems recognizing and expressing his deeper feelings. Therefore, he responds most intensely to a perceptive, intuitive woman, who can help him sort himself out.

He is intensely emotional, but he can also be emotionally detached, and he has the uncanny capability of cutting off his feelings when they interfere with his functioning. Therefore, while he seeks to satisfy his security needs in a love relationship, he can create a nagging sense of insecurity on the part of his mate. His self-obsessive, solitary nature can make a woman feel more like an extracurricular activity than a person who is loved, recognized, and appreciated.

At the same time, while he may not give the woman of his life his total attention, he can be insanely jealous should she let her eyes or body stray. Mr Scorpio tends to be a man whose mind dwells in double standards. While he wants all, he gives a lot less to get it. Essentially he has enough passion to assign it in different areas. However, in turn, he's capable of demanding total devotion and undivided attention.

Sexually, he is intense. However, unless he is emotionally involved, he can be cold, insensitive, and perfunctory. For Mr Scorpio, sex is a psychological as well as physical involvement. Everything he does reflects it. And it shows in a magnetism that makes many women's minds fog up. What it does for a woman's emotions can be devastating, however, when he segregates his feelings from his sexuality. When mature, he can be the very best.

However, one of the many contradictions of his personality is that, while his intelligence may make him old at an early age, his emotions can keep him an infant for a lifetime. But his peculiar danger is that, unlike other adult infants who conspicuously show their warped sensibilities, Mr Scorpio shows only shrewd control. The essential problem in loving him comes in making him lose it. Not only is this not easy, there are many clever Scorpio men with whom it is close to impossible. Until he grows up enough to stop being afraid of his feelings, he will always be at the mercy of them. Likewise, any unsuspecting woman who falls in love with this lower type will find herself controlled by his very fears, his demons, his desires and his decadent way of making life deathlike.

His Good Points

Even during adolescence, he has an avuncular quality and can be counted on in all types of crises. At his best, Mr Scorpio is sympathetic, intuitive, emotionally understanding, and deeply caring. He is a most loyal friend in need who can rise to the dire demands of any occasion. He is also ambitious, powerful, and profoundly intelligent.

His Bad Points

He can be possessive, jealous, sadistic, and downright dishonest. Frequently he suffers from severe mood swings and can have a gloomy, constricted view of life. When pushed past his controls, he can be capable of killing. However, generally he vents his anger through a sarcasm that goes straight to the jugular.

How to Get His Attention

Look cool, sexy and slightly dangerous. Wear something that gives you a sense of power, like a black leather skirt and Chanel No. 5. Don't engage in superficial small talk. It will only annoy him. This is a man who is arrested by a woman who reaches his depths. Therefore, be intense, aware, and also mysterious. When you talk to him, look deep into his eyes and smile alluringly. Ask him out for a drink and then leave abruptly at seven. Let him know you have plans but you'd like to see him again. Before you leave, tell him how attractive you find him. Feed into his obsessive-compulsive mind by keeping him guessing, and you may get to keep him forever.

How to Keep It

Sexually enslave him while you emotionally outmanipulate him. Show up for an impromptu midnight rendezvous in a trench coat, but nothing else. Then be aggressive, and suggest variations. Best of all, let him know that you know what he's all about. If, at this point you're still not certain, it's best not to venture further. Once he senses that you don't understand him, he'll also know that you're in his power, and he'll never appreciate you fully. What he really wants is to be emotionally enslaved. And this comes not only through sex, but through a lot of penetrating insight. Essentially, to keep Mr Scorpio attracted, you have to keep up with him. While that insecure part of him may seek to nurture and control a more shallow woman, he can only be totally consumed by someone he considers his equal. A final point to consider is patience. If he *is* wildly attracted, another part of him will rise up in terror and try in little ways to resist. So be very offhand when he starts to break dates because of the demands of his work. Cheerfully hint that you have other alternatives waiting in the wings. If he thinks that you have nothing better to do than sit back and wait, he'll lose respect and let you sit forever. Therefore, it is equally important not to wait *too* long. If you're really smart and have a lot of self-control, make *him* wait. And as you give him a perfectly plausible reason for breaking a date, make sure that your voice sounds vague. Mr Scorpio always wants something more when he fears he might not be able to have it. So to have him, let him know in little ways that he might not always have you. This will make him miserable. But in a very perverse way, it's this kind of misery that often makes him quite happy.

Realistic Expectations

The ultimate outcome of an involvement with Mr Scorpio depends on how far you want it to go, and on how far he is willing to take it. If you want more than a fling, find out immediately by assessing the pattern of his past relationships. Then observe if he flinches when you speak of the future. Regardless of what he may say, watch what he does. And if he appears confused, totally consumed by his work, or sad because he's consumed by his feelings, then back off and be very cautious.

SAGITTARIUS MAN

November 23–December 21

What He's Like

He is the classic adventurer who seems to be going in several directions simultaneously. Mr Sagittarius is spontaneous and freedom-loving, funny and full of life. He has a childlike kind of charm that can steal your heart away and an innocent little boy grin that may make you want to borrow him for a lifetime.

His is a restless nature that gets bored very easily. And whenever this happens, he is on the move. He loves airports and airplanes, foreign places, and simply playing around. In any given experience he has one foot out the door, moving in the opposite direction. And when the urge to roam overtakes him, neither a grand love nor a sense of responsibility will hold him down. To say the least, he can be maddeningly flighty. But at the same time, he flies through life with an enviable élan.

Mr Sagittarius has a special weakness for a variety of female faces and tends to treat love like a sport, with time-outs and half-times. The basic problem is that he doesn't view much beyond the moment seriously. It often takes him until old age to grow up, and along the way there are quite a few regressions.

Spontaneously he'll make promises he won't keep, extend invitations he'll subsequently forget, and quite innocently stand you up for some more consuming activity. Not only can he be unresponsive to your deeper feelings, he can't stop running long enough to even realize that you have them.

Mr Sagittarius tends to be so superficial that all he sees is your personality and, of course, your good looks and your great sense of humour. This is a man whose loyalties lie in the now and whose priority is pleasure seeking. In so doing, he'll be outrageously generous. And that is basically because money alone has less value than a good time. His head is in the clouds and his feet are always floating, and where he may land, he doesn't particularly want to know.

What He Thinks He Wants

He lusts for adventure, excitement, the unknown, the unexplored, and the yet to be discovered. In general, Mr Sag would prefer many women over a monogamous situation and can change his mind momentarily when it comes to making a commitment. Basically he wants to feel free, unfettered, and fantastically alive. And whether it's a balloon ranch, an impromptu trip to the Azores, or a fabulous new affair, he'll run with it, as fast as he can and as far as he feels he wants it to take him.

What He Needs

He needs to feel that he's free to come and go where he wants, when he wants, with whomever he wants. The feeling of freedom is the source of his jubilation, and jubilation is the drug of his existence. In general, Mr Sag is dampened by the idea of being tied down and tied *into* any situation. Therefore, he can be maddeningly elusive when it comes to either marriage or making a relationship work that may be in trouble. If he had his preference, he would like to live his life ten minutes at a time with the hope that there would always be a new adventure hovering on the horizon.

What He Fears

He fears stagnancy and the feeling that he's chained to a situation that will never change. Basically Mr Sag has such a horror of being restricted that sometimes he can't even show up on time. He has nightmares of suffocation and daydreams of flying high through the sky. Women who want to lean on him terrify him, as do confining situations that feel like they might last forever.

His Attitude Toward Women, Love, and Sex

He has a casual attitude toward sex that rather frequently precludes love. Basically he loves a woman when he's with her. But when he's away from her, whatever happens is another story. Fidelity is not one of his favourite things; nor is having to commit his life away. Essentially, Mr Sag means well, but what he means when he says something is often only good for the moment. Because he has a basic struggle with follow-through, he may invite you to the Bahamas on a Friday, and by Saturday forget that he even mentioned it. This is a man who is not only capable of standing you up, but of behaving like a holy innocent when blamed for his capriciousness. Since 'love them and leave them' is his basic philosophy, he could happily live his life unmarried. Often until old age, his attitude toward love is more playful than passionate, his behaviour flighty, and his feelings cheerful yet uncommitted. When Mr Sag marries early, he is frequently unfaithful. Essentially, it takes him many years to realize that his female partner is also a person with feelings that extend beyond the moment. Unless he is highly evolved, his sense of responsibility is short-sighted, and his behaviour self-centred. However, his enthusiasm is never-ending, and his boyish charm capable of carrying him through even the tighter times.

His Good Points

He's as exuberant as a child with a large red balloon. Likewise, he's not only funny, but a lot of fun. He can make you feel that life is like an exciting safari where all the animals talk and the adventure never ends. Caught in the throes of his wild enthusiasm, Mr Sag is generous to a fault. On impulse he is capable of picking up a dinner tab for ten and then overtipping the waiter. Essentially he is a lovable character whose zest for life and sense of humour make him more exciting than a sailboat on a sunny summer afternoon. At his best, he is wise and philosophical, a benevolent figure who searches beyond convention in a never-ending quest for truth.

His Bad Points

He can be superficial and capricious, flighty and incapable of follow-through. He makes promises he often fails to deliver on. And that's usually because his memory is so bad that he forgets what he promises. Mr Sag has a flaky brain that is capable of forgetting not only where he parked his car, but if he in fact parked it at all. In relationships he finds it a strain to be faithful, especially when surrounded by a bevy of beautiful faces that alter his attention span. Generally speaking, he is far more interested in momentary gratification than in long-range commitments, and even then he is always searching for a few outs. Although he is a charming fellow, it takes him a lifetime to grow up. That is essentially because he is more concerned with playing at life than with sedulously pursuing things with seriousness. And because he can so easily lose interest, he sometimes ends up losing a lot.

How to Get His Attention

Entice him with a startling wit and engaging sense of humour. (It's one of the keys to his attention span.) Early on, let him know you're a completely independent person. To his mind, freedom is like a fanatical religion. Therefore, any signs of a clinging vine will send him scurrying in the farthest direction. He's got to know that you'll do very well without him before he'll allow himself to be attracted. Appeal to his love of nature by suggesting a hike or help on an ecology fund-raiser. However, keep in mind that this is a guy who would prefer to scale glaciers and windsurf in the rain than take a mild little walk in the woods. Be prepared to do anything at any moment. Mr Sagittarius is very spontaneous. Also, go light with the makeup. Mr Sag prefers a natural look to lots of glamour and frowns upon too much primping and fussing for the sake of presenting your face to the world.

How to Keep It

Give him so much freedom that he feels like he's living in an airport. When, not *if*, he gets you angry, show him that you have both the spunk and the self-assurance to put him in his place. In the surrounding moments seduce his personality with your sense of humour, and then go after his body. He only needs a little encouragement to divert his energy reserves; if you can keep up with him, he'll be yours – but there's no guarantee for how long. Let him know quite firmly that there are limitations to what you'll allow him to get away with. If you let Mr Sag scamper over you, he'll cheerfully fly right out of your life. At the same time, if you scream and complain, in record time he'll be purchasing a plane ticket. The best way to keep him is to spell out your expectations. Then let him know that if he is too much of a child to enjoy treating you like a person, you're capable of cutting out in record time. Never rely on subtlety to get a point across. He's much too dense to notice, never mind understand. Finally, during the courtship, should he begin to behave capriciously, either stand him up or keep him waiting. Then coolly inquire how it feels to be on the other side.

Realistic Expectations

Although Mr Sag is a lot of fun, he's far more of a fling than a lasting love affair. Basically this is because his idea of settling down is seeing someone else on the side. Not only can he not be confined, he often can't be counted upon. As a friend you may find him loyal, alive, and amusing. However, emotionally he has a long way to go as a lover. If you're merely interested in a good time, he is a man who can give it to you. But if you want something more than the morning after, don't hold your breath or you won't be breathing for very long.

Capricorn Man

December 22–January 20

What He's Like

He takes everything in life seriously, including things that happen to be funny. Even when he's joking around, Mr Capricorn is a very serious man. Romantically he tends to be shy and unsure of himself, even though he can command the highest position of power in the business world. Capricorn is the apogee of ambition. From the time that he was a small child, he decided that he would be no ordinary man.

Not only is he goal-orientated, he has a drive that would shame the average superachiever. Mr Capricorn is the original workaholic, and his price for putting in his total time on a project is pervasive material reward. Unlike Virgo, praise from the boss simply isn't enough. Capricorn wants to not only be the boss but to be paid handsomely for it.

Money is so important that he probably had a savings account at the age of seven, which accrued from mowing lawns when everyone else was playing baseball. Because he is so emotionally insecure, he makes up for it by counting his pennies, nickels, and dollar bills. However, although he can be both frugal and parsimonious, he is capable of spending lavishly on items that will improve his self-image, like an elegant apartment, a Rolex, or a very expensive car. Since Mr Capricorn is highly status-oriented, he is continually conscious of how things appear from the outside. Therefore, he is most attracted to women of highly dignified bearing who also look good to the world.

Although this man sports an exceptionally tough exterior, underneath he is as vulnerable as an adolescent with acne. Capricorn will go to any lengths to protect his self-image. And because he hates to admit to any kind of weakness, at times he will withdraw and appear very cold.

Discipline, grit, and tenacity are his gods, and he would like to believe that they will take him anywhere. Quite often they do, but at the expense of his sensitivity. Mr Capricorn needs to develop the feminine side of his nature, and until he does, he runs the risk of being rigid and cold.

There is a strongly pessimistic side to his personality that makes him cautious, calculating, anxious, and depressive. He can be as gloomy as a rainy day and terribly moody. Instead of hoping for the best, he often fears the worst and sometimes makes life seem like a series of chores.

At the same time, not only is he conscientious, he is also highly responsible. It could be that Mr Capricorn invented follow-through. Once he makes a commitment, it can be depended on, regardless of the problems it might cause in his life. Likewise he can be a stern taskmaster with other people, since he often has expectations that exceed most people's limits. However, when Mr Capricorn occasionally allows himself to lighten up, he can bring to life a courage that commands.

What He Thinks He Wants

He wants security and power, both material and emotional. Even with five million in the bank, Mr Capricorn may be concerned that there isn't enough money for emergencies. Emotionally, he desires a woman he can depend on. And in any serious relationship, he wants to feel pampered, admired, and catered to. Emotional power is his driving force, the achievement of it his raison d'etre. Nothing else will ease his anxiety and offer him a total sense of well-being.

What He Needs

Power and *control* are the key words to his personality. And he will drive himself to any lengths to attain them. Because on a very deep-seated level he is so insecure, he needs to dictate to others to assure himself that he is the man he would like to be. In a business situation, he will pull the strings from behind the scenes, and in a romantic situation, he will offer endless suggestions in regard to what should be. Once he is in control, Mr Capricorn feels positively defined. And that is probably his favourite feeling.

What He Fears

His primal fears are rejection and conspicuous loss of dignity. Mr Capricorn is overly obsessed with his self-image and the role that he plays to the world. Whether he is running a business or a marathon, he wants to both look and be at his best. Essentially, he has to show the world that he's boss, even if he really feels like a little boy.

His Attitude Toward Women, Love, and Sex

Unless he has a strongly placed Uranus in his chart, this is not a man who will fall in love on sight or even overnight. Mr Capricorn is cautious. And in addition to that, he's also shy. Still further, he has to decide whether you're worthy of his serious attention. And that alone can take him some time.

Because he cares terribly about how he appears to the world, he will want a woman who will in some way enhance him. However, at the same time, because deep down he is insecure, his compliments can come out almost sounding like criticism.

In all respects Mr Capricorn's approach to life is conservative. And this also applies to the way he views women. This is a man who is convinced that women must not only know their place, but must remain there. Because at all times he needs to feel in control, he can't bear competition, just as he can't bear coming in second place to a pretty face.

Although he may not prevent a woman from working, basically he believes that women should be wives and mothers, that he should be the breadwinner, and that nobody should dispute the situation. As a breadwinner, he'll be the best. There will be two cars in the driveway, a comfortable home in the suburbs, and a very large savings account in the bank. Although Mr Capricorn is not the most exciting man in the zodiac, he is at the same time very secure. He has a strongly chauvinistic streak, but he is always dependable. And while his ego may have a hard time accepting a woman as at least an equal, if broached to him in the most diplomatic way, he might try. However, the attitude that he most easily falls back on is 'Don't worry your little head about all of these life essentials. Just do as I tell you, and everything will be more than fine.'

Although he is the marrying type, he is not the kind of man who will appreciate taking second place to any of your interests. At all given times, he wants to know your whereabouts, just as he wants to be assured that you're not doing anything you shouldn't be. Mr Capricorn can be uncontrollably jealous. However, rather than openly admitting it, he'll grow cold, remote, and very grumpy. Essentially, his least favourite thing is feeling vulnerable, because it depletes his sense of power and quickly eliminates his control.

Because he is far more pragmatic than romantic, he is likely to forget the flowers, not even consider the champagne, and bring you to a restaurant that is not only reasonable in price but known *only* for good food. However, after you have really won him, he'll present you with a fur – if he thinks it makes you look good, himself more powerful, and your relationship more lustrous to the outside world.

There are worse men than Mr Capricorn when it comes to loving. However, the inherent contradiction in his character is that he can be insensitive to your feelings, while he still takes you very seriously.

His Good Points

He is dependable, conscientious, dedicated, and enduring. Mr Capricorn thrives on responsibility and achieving certain goals that would intimidate the average person. In a very quiet way, he can take charge of an entire situation, business, or person. He is a strong, serious man who can be called upon when needed and then will come through with flying colours.

His Bad Points

He can be an insensitive snob who never sees beyond the superficial. Power can become his god, and money the means of attaining it. The lowly evolved Capricorn man is capable of coldly using anyone to get what he wants, and he'll justify it by the degree of his desire. He can debase a deep trust and treat people like objects who were put in his path merely for his self-interest. And after he has performed his dishonest deeds, he will cover himself with a lot of self-righteous attitudes that he works hard at actually believing.

How to Get His Attention

He is a die-hard conservative who looks down his nose on flash. So wear something classic bur expensive like suede and cashmere. (His values are very materialistic – he is easily impressed with price tags.) Under your clothes wear black, sexy underwear. He doesn't have to see it; you'll know it's there and it will give you a psychological edge. Since Mr Capricorn takes his self-image so seriously, he can't tell flattery from compliments and can never get enough of either. So flatter him on the quality of his clothes, his important position, or his extraordinary competence which has won your respect. Mr Capricorn adores feeling powerful and respected. Put on a show and watch this masculine leader take charge.

How to Keep It

Make him feel admired, appreciated, respected, and desired. Although on the surface he may appear like a power mogul, underneath he seeks the love and attention of a child. Essentially he needs a woman who will question neither his authority nor his demands. During his murky moments of depression, he will depend on your support. Nurture him, but don't lose your identity. Reassure him of his power at the same time that you make him aware that you are more than a mere extension of his life. Don't be shy about being sexually aggressive. At the same time let him know how much you love being with him – everywhere – and how much pleasure he gives you. Finally, never let him take your kindness for granted, even if he bears tidings of expensive trinkets before he turns his back because of the demands of his busy business life.

Realistic Expectations

Mr Capricorn can be a serious and responsible mate if you play the relationship the way he wants it. For women who simply want to be taken care of, he is a present from the clouds. However, for a woman who is dedicated to her career or to a consuming interest, considerable friction could arise from his need for control. Although he can be a bastion of support for someone insecure, for a freedom-loving woman he can be suffocating. Unlike Mr Libra, Mr Capricorn is not open to objective discussions about how both can better a bad situation. Not only is he rigid about the fact that he wants things his way, but to support his position, he has an exhausting number of reasons.

Aquarius Man

January 21–February 19

What He's Like

He's a friendly kind of fellow who's interested in everybody and everything – at least a little. Mr Aquarius is defined by his curiosity and sometimes by his curiousness. In an impersonal way, he would like to commune with every force in the universe, and he spends much of his life trying.

His favourite thing is getting inside people's heads to find out what they're thinking and why. He is delighted by the novelty of experience and intrigued by the unconventional.

And his mind will never stop until he has thoroughly explored the nature of it all.

Since Mr Aquarius is far more mental than emotional, he sometimes treats people more as abstractions than as feeling beings, and revels in making theories on their behaviour. Analysis can be his nemesis, especially when he makes a person feel somewhat like a psychiatric patient with a fascinating mental disorder.

He has an enthusiasm for gossip and an unsurpassed interest in other people's peculiarities. Often it would seem that he is more interested in everybody else's life than in his own. And this can pose some problems, especially in his love relationships.

Essentially, Mr Aquarius likes many things and people in many different ways. For him, every individual has relative value. However, because he makes everything so relative, he looks at very little as absolute. And that, of course, includes love.

He's about as difficult to pin down as a crazed butterfly, and a definite challenge when it comes to commitment. Whether it is a career, an interest, or a romantic interlude, Mr Aquarius will always have other things going on at the same time. He is a freedom-loving fellow who loves to dabble and drift about in ideas, people, and projects. However, how far he is willing to take anything can sometimes be a very mysterious matter.

Allowed to go his own way, Mr Aquarius will cheerfully float through space, sometimes theorizing about life rather than living it. However, although he is emotionally detached, he isn't unfeeling. Not only is he a friend in need, he can also be the kind of humanitarian who sacrifices his own interests for those of a group. Most of the time, he is an idealist who is more concerned with how life should be and might be than how it is.

Such a man may be fascinating yet maddening to fall in love with, especially when you feel that your interests come after both his friends' and his ideals. And because Mr Aquarius considers everyone from cab drivers to cocktail waitresses his 'friends,' the competition can get quite heavy, not to mention highly emotional, Watch him talk intensely to some seductive beauty and then talk yourself into believing that he was only interested in her emotional problems. The extraordinary thing is that he probably was.

Mr Aquarius believes in honesty and communication above all else. And although he may appear like a flirt, he's far more interested in finding out how someone's mind ticks. Essentially, his definition of freedom is being able to experience a lot of different people in a lot of different ways. However, his way is usually far more mental than emotional or sexual

Although he is a group person, Mr Aquarius is also a loner. At regular intervals he seeks solitude, and at all times he needs his space. Easily made claustrophobic, he is terrified of being closed in upon by anything or anyone, and at any time. He is everyone's friend, yet no one's inseparable buddy. And even in love, he watches his life from afar, as if it were something quite apart from him that he happens to find fascinating.

What He Thinks He Wants

Ideally he would like to have an interchange with everyone in the world, and then formulate a theory on each person's behaviour. He loves to have a lot of people around him to communicate with, just as he loves the freedom to move from person to person. However, what he would like most from the encounter with each person is to learn something so new and fascinating that he forgets what day it is.

What He Needs

He needs freedom at all costs. A caged Aquarian is like an athlete without legs. Space, both physical and psychological, is crucial to his existence, and every day must feel as if it has the potential to be totally different from the preceding one.

What He Fears

He fears stagnancy, the absence of change, and being boxed in in any situation. At all times Mr Aquarius must feel free to roam, experiment, and experience. To him, every experience is an experience worth having – at least once. However, what he considers even worse than death is being caught in a rut with no way out in sight and no hope that there ever will be.

His Attitude Toward Women, Love, and Sex

Mr Aquarius is far more of an interesting companion than a passionate lover. And that's because, on a very impersonal level, he can love a lot of people.

Essentially Mr Aquarius would rather spend the night engaged in a stimulating conversation than make love until dawn. Therefore, he is more enthralled with a woman whose mind is a turn-on than with a glamour girl who has nothing to say.

However, because he is so freedom-loving and dispassionate, emotional commitments are not easily forthcoming. With him, you have to take it slow. In the meantime, he may discuss past and present girlfriends in your presence, and in the process make you feel like a movie extra. Falling in love with Mr Aquarius is not easy for someone emotional. Especially when he discusses laser beams over candlelight, rather than complimenting you on your beauty or your cooking. Later on, when you're thinking of making love, in his friendly manner he'll inform you that he doesn't believe in commitment, that security is illusion, and the he loves women because they make such fantastic friends. The greatest compliment that can come from Mr Aquarius is that he likes your mind. Second to that is that he finds you terribly interesting to talk to. Therefore, if you happen to be searching for the kind of breathless romance that might make you forget what day it is here, do not hold your breath. This is not to imply that he doesn't mean well. Or that he will never marry. However, because he sees beyond society's structures and likes so many people in different ways, a monogamous commitment will be a long time coming. Mr Aquarius can't stand to be closed in on. And not only that, he won't be.

If you are interesting enough to intrigue him, it is likely that he will analyze almost everything you do and say. Not only is he perceptive, but he tends to file away his observations in his brain, and at maddening times, will coolly produce a 'fact' or theory. During what could ostensibly pass as a romantic moment, he will not turn to you and whisper that you turn him on. Rather it is much more likely that he will ask you why you happen to like a certain colour. Not only is Mr Aquarius cool, he is also very curious.

However, although he is cool, he is not uncaring. He is the first person to help you move ten years of possessions up a five-flight walk-up – without complaining. Or he will cheerfully take your temperature and make you tea and toast when you are sick. (Aquarian men make wonderful doctors.) Yet just as you are sinking securely into your bed pillows and feeling truly pampered, the phone will ring. It will be one of his old girlfriends calling to ask a favour. And can Mr Aquarius refuse? Of course not. Tenderly he'll kiss you on the forehead and tell you that he'll be back some-time later that afternoon, but not to be worried if he doesn't show up until midnight. And can you trust him? Yes. Deep in his heart, Mr Aquarius is much less like a playboy and more like a holy innocent. Keep that in mind as the door shuts.

His Good Points

He is honest, objective, and often brilliant. He has a mind that sees beyond its time, and often an advanced under-standing of life and people. Mr Aquarius is not confined by his ego, but rather rises beyond it in a perpetual search for the truth.

His Bad Points

He can be cold and analytical, emotionally erratic and capricious. At times, Mr Aquarius can be insensitive to the feelings of others and may use a situation or a person merely for his own gain, Since game playing comes so easily to him, he can sometimes be tempted to manipulate a situation in his favour.

How to Get His Attention

This man is galvanized by brilliance, the far out, the unique and unusual. He's a thinker who is ahead of his time, and the key to his soul is his mind. A woman with an extraordinary mentality is far more seductive to Mr Aquarius than any beauty queen. To really get his attention, you need brilliant ideas, progressive interests, and fascinating theories, or be a serious follower of some humanitarian cause. Feed his imagination, but don't be sexually threatening. Should the physical outweigh the mental, he'll get bored. Educate your mind and encourage his ideas. If you turn on his mind, he won't care what you're wearing. He would rather be blinded by your words than by your beauty.

How to Keep It

Wait for him to win your trust, then don't confine him. Let him feel free to attend an impromptu lecture on asteroids, and don't overreact if he wants to keep in touch with his old girlfriends. If something he is doing bothers you, he is a man who is open to reasonable discussions. Mr Aquarius was made for communicating. Therefore, if you feel a sudden impasse, it's probably because you're not confronting him. At all times, let him know what you're feeling and thinking, and why. Essentially, his ideal is not a sex goddess, but an independent woman with a great mind and character, whose intelligence makes her simply marvellous to talk to.

Realistic Expectations

If you are seeking a grand emotional-sexual passion, forget it. At best, Mr Aquarius will be your best friend. And that's not so bad! However, if you are terribly insecure, uncontrollably jealous, or looking for a man who is merely a bastion of security, look elsewhere. Mr Aquarius believes in give and take, and he wants an equal partner who will respond to the world in the same way he does. However, if you are the type of woman who is titillated by a progressive intellect and you have a lot of interests and ideas of your own, this could be a match that soars beyond the stars.

Pisces Man

February 20–March 20

What He's Like

He's an ethereal dreamer with romantic desires and secret longings. Mr Pisces is a mystical kind of man who sees the universe not as it is, but as he would like it. He has the soul of a poet in search of splendour. And he will take it wherever he can find it, be it in the form of art, alcohol, drugs, sex, or his fantasies.

He tends to be an escapist who has problems confronting whatever makes him uncomfortable and so communicates through noncommunication. Even when he is completely honest, it often seems that there is a great deal left unsaid. Hence, it is frequently difficult to understand where he's coming from, what he wants, and where he wants to go. And it is likely that even he doesn't know himself since he spends a great deal of time writhing in his own confusion.

Basically his favourite feeling is infatuation, accompanied by all the sensual delights of a new love. Yet when it comes to the grosser mundane matters (like taking out the garbage), Mr Pisces would rather quietly retreat with a book.

There are Piscean men who are moguls in the business world; however, their true nature probably yearns for some type of artistic expression. Whether he expresses it or not, the Pisces man is intensely creative, intuitive, and sometimes psychic. He has compassion for the underprivileged, is a silent champion of the underdog and a committed believer in the creation of a utopia. Regardless of his exterior, his inner nature is sensitive and emotional, his mind sympathetic, and his intentions good. However, the problem is that because he tends to spend so much time in his own head, his behaviour can also be self-centred and his actions insensitive. Mr Pisces' problem is that he needs to be enslaved by his feelings, and whether they are fear, love, desire, or depression, they will dictate the man and he will move to their beat. Therefore, although he can quickly fall in love, he can just as quickly run away from love when he feels pressured. This inconstant behaviour can prove quite puzzling to a person who five days before was the object of such exuberant enthusiasm. However, Mr Pisces would probably never consider his behaviour confusing, since he doesn't really want to think about it. All he knows is that anything that feels unpleasant must be escaped from. And due to a lot of practice, he does his escaping so cleverly that one might even think he's still there.

What He Thinks He Wants

He wants to be totally swept away through sensual pleasure and the emotional power of a great love. Mr Pisces has the soul of a poet who seeks enraptured experience. Ideally he would like to live in the fourth dimension, where all experience is like a divine high and he is never bothered by the blight of boredom.

What He Needs

He needs intellectual, emotional, and sensual excitement –
the more the better, the longer, the more divine.

What He Fears

Boredom, routine, tedium, and stagnancy have a debilitating effect on his psyche and probably account for his worst fears. To alleviate the experience of monotony, he seeks escapes in the form of artistic experience, drugs, alcohol, sex, or mysticism. And in a crowded elevator, he'll simply go inside his head. Because there are a lot of things in life that he does not want to see or hear. Mr Pisces sees only what he wants to see and has a very clever habit of creating his own scripts. Therefore, when you are with him and look in his eyes and know that he's not really with you, it's most likely because there's a movie going on in his mind – and it's probably in Technicolor.

His Attitude Toward Women, Love, and Sex

Mr Pisces is an ethereal romantic who can fall in love in five minutes and out of love in about four. Essentially, he loves women. However, what entrances him even more than the most beautiful woman is the power of the emotion he is capable of feeling for her. Like Mr Aquarius, Mr Pisces can love a lot of women in a lot of different ways. However, unlike the detached Aquarian man, his emotions are much more dramatic.

He is a dreamer who is in love with the drama of emotion. He lives for sensation, scenes of emotional rapture, and erotic flights of fantasy. And when it all wears off, it is likely that his attention will drift elsewhere.

There are Pisces men who settle into one relationship, never to stray from the side of their partner. But it is likely that they fantasize a lot. Yet one will never know for sure, since this is a mysterious man who never reveals himself completely.

However, it can be said that this sign is associated with a high incidence of affairs, both before and during marriage.

And during marriage, Mr Pisces can have a more populated love life than many men who are single. However, the irony of the situation is that of all the signs of the zodiac, he might be the least sexually aggressive.

Because he is not a man who goes out of his way, when Mr Pisces has affairs, it's because the situation presents itself. It might be mentioned that, quite mysteriously, situations always present themselves – perhaps because he is ever alert to all possibilities. And since he has such a friendly way of approaching and then turning passive, women often feel compelled to make the first move.

Therefore, Mr Pisces has sly and highly successful ways of gratifying his desires. However, it might be said that not only does he feel for all of his women after each show is over, he would like them all to hang around as friends. Mr Pisces prides himself on his sympathetic nature, as well as on the fact that most of his old flames still stay in touch. Yet the most puzzling contradiction of his character is that for a man who can be so emotional, he can also be surprisingly detached and impersonal.

Essentially he carries around a lot of universal love in his heart, which enables him to distance himself from the needs of his own ego. Should the love of his life suddenly tell him that she wants him to meet her secret lover, not only will he not be angry, but he'll do his best to understand. And if upon reflection he comes to the understanding that his competitor might make her more happy, quite nobly he will simply disappear. It might be noted that it is almost impossible to make Mr Pisces jealous. While he may in a moment of passion murmur that he'll sacrifice his life for you, he'll never go down in your history as someone who will fight for your love. It's more likely that he'll merely float on to his next affair or fantasy, musing about how much he appreciates your friendship.

Sexually, he tends to be passive and prefers that the woman make most of the moves. While he'll keep up his part enthusiastically, Mr Pisces is far more of a follower than an initiator. Therefore, he's most comfortable with aggressive women who take over, while he floats off in his head.

When it comes to marriage, he is a man who is a challenge to pin down. Since the idea of a snug domestic domicile directly conflicts with his need for romantic drama, it is likely that he will postpone the discussion of marriage for as long as possible, until he hopes that you've simply forgotten. If that doesn't work, he may reluctantly respond to begging and badgering. But the price for this is that while he may go through the motions of getting married, he may simultaneously pretend that none of it is really happening. It is a fact that Mr Pisces can be quite an enigma. At the same time he can appear innocent, charming, and very lovable. In his own heart, he's loyal, since he sees loyalty as a matter of loving, not owning. And any way you look at it, Mr Pisces can love even more than a lot.

His Good Points

He can be kind, caring, and very sympathetic – especially in a situation involving some emotional distance. Mr Pisces is highly intuitive, imaginative, artistic, and romantic. When in love, he will make you believe that you're his greatest love. He will draw you into his fantasy and excite you to feel that you're seventeen years old and falling in love for the first time. He has a very special talent for creating a larger-than-life romance. And that is because he can make a woman feel that suddenly her life is like a lovely piece of music.

His Bad Points

He can be hypocritical, dishonest, manipulative, sarcastic, and maddeningly passive. The less-evolved Piscean man is an escapist addicted to divine highs. Drugs, alcohol, and sex are his raison d'etre. Essentially, he lives his life for sensation and takes no responsibility when his dreams turn into destructive traps that bring sorrow not only to himself, but to everyone else around him.

How to Get His Attention

Charm him and appeal to the child inside him. Mr Pisces loves to play and have his imagination fed. Because he craves stimulation rather than security, you should present yourself with an air of drama and excitement. Wear something wonderful that makes you feel like a goddess. He is sensitive to colour, so create some striking visuals. He is also susceptible to moods and atmospheres, so set up a dinner where the champagne flows freely. Be witty, amusing, and intent on entertaining him. However, also keep in mind that he is more interested in a fantasy than a real woman with needs and demands. So go light on reality while you maintain a degree of emotional distance at all times. The more of the sexy, unattainable ice maiden you are, the more ardent he'll become.

How to Keep It

This part is not that easy, since his mind and emotions tend to wander. To capture his total attention, you have to keep up the splendour of the romance. Make every day different and every night a romantic drama. Convince him that his life is greater than the Great Gatsby's by providing constant excitement and playing the role of his great love. In the meantime, make sure you're not always available when he calls. Always make him work to please you, since he will appreciate you more when you keep him on his toes. Never let him forget the power you have over him, and he'll be your ardent admirer for as long as you want him.

Realistic Expectations

Because this man is a mystery, even to himself, it is difficult to predict not only what he will do but why. At times it may seem like you're giving a lot and getting very little back. At other times, his words may convince you that you have him while his actions tell you that you don't have a chance. Because Mr Pisces can be so passive, he can make you feel that you're producing, directing, and acting alone in your own romantic drama. And due to his elusive personality, it could be that you are. This is a relationship that should be put through a benefit-cost analysis. Carefully evaluate what it is you want versus what you're getting versus what you're giving. And above all, if you're not getting, don't fall into the trap of thinking one day you will be. Mr Pisces will not change – unless perhaps he leaves your life for another woman.